Internet links

Throughout this book, we have recommended interesting websites where you can find out more about the Victorians. To visit the recommended sites, go to the Usborne Quicklinks Website at **www.usborne-quicklinks.com** and type the keyword "Victorians". There you will find links to click on to take you to all the sites. Here are some of the things you can do on the recommended sites:

• Read extracts from Queen Victoria's diary.
• Find out more about living conditions in Victorian workhouses.
• Take a virtual tour around Joseph Paxton's Crystal Palace.
• Look at original illustrations from Victorian children's books.

Internet safety

When using the Internet, please make sure you follow these guidelines:

• Ask your parent or guardian for permission before you connect to the Internet.
• When you are on the Internet, never tell anyone your full name, address or telephone number, and ask an adult before you give your email address.
• If a website asks you to log in or register by typing your name or email address, ask an adult's permission first.
• If you do receive an email from someone you don't know, tell an adult and do not reply to the email.

COMPUTER NOT ESSENTIAL

If you don't have access to the Internet, don't worry. This book is a complete, self-contained reference book on its own.

Site availability

The links in Usborne Quicklinks are regularly reviewed and updated, but occasionally you may get a message that a site is unavailable. This might be temporary, so try again later, or even the next day. If any of the sites close down, we will, if possible, replace them with suitable alternatives, so you will always find an up-to-date list of sites in Usborne Quicklinks.

What you need

Most websites listed in this book can be accessed using a standard home computer and a web browser (the software that lets you look at information from the Internet). Some sites need extra programs (plug-ins) to play sound or show videos or animations. If you go to a site and do not have the necessary plug-in, a message will come up on the screen. There is usually a button on the site that you can click on to download the plug-in. Alternatively, go to Usborne Quicklinks and click on **Net Help**. There, you can find links to download plug-ins.

Notes for parents and guardians

The websites described in this book are regularly reviewed and the links in Usborne Quicklinks are updated. However, the content of a website may change at any time and Usborne Publishing is not responsible for the content on any website other than its own. We recommend that children are supervised while on the Internet, that they do not use Internet chat rooms, and that you use Internet filtering software to block unsuitable material. Please ensure that your children read and follow the safety guidelines printed on the left. For more information, see the "Net Help" area on the Usborne Quicklinks Website.

The illustration opposite is from the first edition of Charles Dickens's *A Christmas Carol*, which was published in 1843-44.

VICTORIANS

Ruth Brocklehurst

Designed by Stephen Wright

Edited by Jane Chisholm

Consultant: Professor Hilary Fraser
Birkbeck College, University of London

Queen Victoria's family tree

This family tree shows four generations of Queen Victoria's family. The dates show the years of each monarch's reign.

GEORGE III
(1760-1820)
= Sophia Charlotte of Mecklenburg-Strelitz

GEORGE IV (1820-1830) = Caroline (daughter of Duke of Brunswick-Wolfenbuttel)

Frederick, Duke of York

WILLIAM IV (1830-1837) = Adelaide (daughter of Duke of Saxe-Meiningen)

Charlotte, Princess Royal

Edward, Duke of Kent = Victoria of Saxe-Coburg

10 others

Charlotte (died in childbirth, with no surviving children) = Leopold of Saxe-Coburg, later King of the Belgians

VICTORIA (1837-1901) = Albert, Duke of Saxe-Coburg-Gotha

Victoria, Princess Royal = Kaiser Friedrich of Germany

Alice = Louis, Grand Duke of Hesse

Helena = Prince Christian of Schleswig-Holstein

Arthur, Duke of Connaught = Princess Louise of Prussia

Beatrice = Prince Henry of Battenberg

EDWARD VII (1901-1910) = Princess Alexandra of Denmark

Alfred, Duke of Edinburgh = Grand Duchess Marie Alexandrovna of Russia

Louise = John Campbell, Duke of Argyll

Leopold, Duke of Albany = Princess Helena of Waldeck

This painting shows Queen Victoria and Prince Albert with their five eldest children.

Contents

Internet links

Look for the Internet links throughout this book. These are descriptions of websites where you can find out more about the Victorians. For a link to these websites, go to **www.usborne-quicklinks.com** and type in the keyword "Victorians".

This is the Prince Albert Memorial, in London, designed for Queen Victoria by the architect George Gilbert Scott. When it was built, it was the most expensive granite and marble structure of its time.

The Victorian age

When 18-year-old Victoria became Queen of Great Britain and Ireland in 1837, she was about to become Britain's longest reigning monarch. She ruled for 64 years, over one of the most exciting periods in British history. Although many people still lived in abject poverty, the Victorian age was one of unstoppable social, economic and scientific progress. By the Queen's death in 1901, Britain had become the wealthiest, most powerful nation in the world.

Shifting power

In 1837, public opinion of the monarchy was at an all time low. Victoria's predecessors had been unpopular – George IV was wasteful and sleazy and William IV was old and doddery. Their reigns saw public protests and bloody riots, as workers demanded better pay and more rights. Some people even thought Britain might be on the brink of a revolution.

Daily life

In the late 18th century, most British people still lived a rural life, working as farmers or spinning wool and cotton to weave into cloth. But, soon new machines were invented that could do these jobs in a fraction of the time. This left many people out of work, so they flocked to the towns in search of jobs in new industries. This radical change in the way people lived and worked became known as the Industrial Revolution. During Victoria's reign, the population more than doubled. By 1901 there were 40 million people in Britain and 75% of them lived in rapidly expanding industrial towns and cities.

This painting, of crowds at a busy railway station, was painted by William Powell Frith in 1862. It is typical of paintings of the time, which often depicted the hustle and bustle of everyday life in Victorian Britain.

The age of empire

During the 19th century, the British acquired an empire, with lands as far apart as Canada, South Africa, India and the Far East. The empire covered a fifth of the world's land and held over 370 million people. It was also an enormous source of wealth and prosperity, as Britain traded goods with the rest of the world from every corner of the empire.

This is Queen Victoria with Abdul Karim, her *munchi*, or advisor, on all Indian issues.

Victorian values

The term "Victorian" is sometimes used to describe people who are are stuffy and old-fashioned. It's true that in a rapidly changing world, many Victorians placed great value on hard work, good manners and family life. But, they were also very forward thinking and enthusiastically welcomed the discoveries and new technologies of the time.

Internet links

For a link to a website where you can watch an animation about some great Victorian achievements, go to **www.usborne-quicklinks.com**

Did you know? Victoria didn't just give her name to a period in British history. A number of cities and landmarks around the world, including lakes and waterfalls, are named after her, too.

Queen Victoria

People often picture Queen Victoria as she was in the last years of her reign, a grumpy, disapproving old lady, but this was far from true of the teenage queen. Although Victoria always took her royal duties very seriously, her personal diaries show that she was passionate and fun-loving too. As a young queen, she enjoyed dressing up in bright silks for the opera and attending lavish balls at Buckingham Palace.

Early years

Victoria was born in Kensington Palace, in London, in 1819 and christened Alexandrina Victoria. Her father, Edward, son of King George III, died when she was a baby. As her uncles, George IV and William IV, had no heirs, it soon became clear that Victoria would succeed William to the throne. The young heiress had a strict, lonely upbringing, with little company apart from her over-protective mother and governess. Despite her solitude, Victoria was a lively, playful child who enjoyed painting, riding, music and dancing.

At four, Victoria, like all children of the time, was dressed as a miniature adult.

Learning to be queen

As well as the usual school subjects such as history and mathematics, Victoria had to learn how to act like royalty. She even had holly leaves tied under her chin to make her hold her head up high. She also had to keep a special book, where she noted everything she did. The book showed that although she was anxious to be good, Victoria was often stubborn and quick-tempered too.

Here, Victoria, seated in the middle and dressed in black, is surrounded by the royal families of Europe.

Public image

When Victoria became queen in 1837, she was determined to restore the image of the monarchy. So it was vital that she made a good impression at her first major public event – her coronation. It was a splendid, dignified affair. During the ceremony, an elderly baron tripped near the throne and Victoria helped him to his feet. This kind gesture won the people's hearts, convincing them that their new queen would be caring, humble and respectable. To them, she became known as England's rose.

This painting of the young Queen Victoria, with a rose in her hand, is by Franz Xavier Winterhalter. He painted more than 120 portraits of Victoria and her family.

Family ties

One of Victoria's duties was to marry and produce an heir. Since most of the royal families of Europe were related, she was likely to marry a relation. When Victoria was 21, she married her German cousin, Albert, Duke of Saxe-Coburg-Gotha, and they had nine children. Later, she urged her children to marry European royalty too, in the hope that family ties would ensure peace. But sadly this proved unsuccessful. When the First World War broke out in 1914, two of her grandsons, King George V and Kaiser Wilhelm II of Germany, were on opposing sides.

Internet links

For links to websites where you can see pictures of Queen Victoria throughout her life and read extracts from her diary, go to **www.usborne-quicklinks.com**

 Did you know? Victoria's first language was German, as that was what her German mother and governess spoke at home. As a child, she even spoke English with a German accent.

The age of steam

This Victorian painting shows a converter, invented by Bessemer to convert iron into steel.

The Industrial Revolution rapidly gained pace during Victoria's reign and its driving force was the power of steam. The first effective steam engines were developed in the 18th century, but Victorian engineers developed bigger, faster, more powerful engines that could run whole factories. This extra power led to a massive increase in the quantity and variety of manufactured goods made in Britain, enabling the Victorians to dominate world trade.

Raw materials

Coal and iron were the raw materials that made the Industrial Revolution possible. Coal was burned in vast furnaces to boil water for steam, and most tools and machines were made from iron. In 1856, Henry Bessemer invented a method for converting iron into steel quickly, cheaply and in bulk. As steel is lighter, stronger and less brittle than iron, this revolutionized British engineering. Ships, bridges, buildings and machinery could now be bigger and more technically advanced than ever before.

Rain, steam and speed – the Great Western Railway, painted in 1839-1844 by J.M.W. Turner, conveys some of the excitement of the new age of steam.

On track

The invention of steam locomotives – engines that moved – also had a phenomenal impact on industrial growth. Trains provided a quick, efficient way to transport raw materials and finished goods, allowing productivity to increase sharply and taking manufactured goods to a wider market. By the end of the 19th century, over 29,000km (18,000 miles) of steel track had been forged and laid, criss-crossing the entire country.

 Did you know? Henry Bessemer patented 150 of his inventions, including an anti-seasickness cabin for a steam ship which was so heavy, it made the ship impossible to steer.

Working life

As the wheels of industry turned, more and more people found work in the mines, factories and shipyards. But industrialization brought appalling working conditions. Workers, including thousands of children as young as 6 years old, were often expected to work for up to 12 hours a day in places that were noisy, polluted and dangerous. Over time, the government introduced a number of laws, enforcing a minimum age for child workers, limiting the number of hours people should work and setting safety standards.

This photograph from 1865 shows a group of shipyard bosses in "stove pipe" hats. Behind them is a large ship in construction and the typical belching chimneys of steelworks and dockside factories.

Workshop of the world

During Victorian times, industrial output was so great that Britain became known as the workshop of the world. By the 1850s, more than half the world's cotton and textile goods were made in the huge mills and factories that sprang up across the north of England and Scotland. And in the major ports – especially where there was good access to coal and steel – trade and shipbuilding grew at an even greater rate. By the 1890s, over 75% of all the ships in the world were British-built.

Internet links

For a link to a website where you can play a game and find out more about the industrial revolution, go to **www.usborne-quicklinks.com**

City life

In 1837, Britain was still a rural nation, with 80% of the people living in the countryside. But, as industry grew, people moved to find work in the factories. By 1850 more than half the population lived in towns and cities. Most factory workers lived in dirty, crowded parts of the town, known as slums.

Life in the slums

Many factory workers were paid very poorly and lived in tiny houses in the slums, with no toilets or running water. The air was thick with smoke from the factories and the streets were filthy, so diseases spread rapidly. There was a lot of crime, because some people had to steal for food or money to survive.

This scene shows part of a British town around 1850.

Thick smoke from factories pollutes the air.

Up to 20 people live in each tiny house.

A chimney sweep

A policeman chasing a pickpocket

People get their water from a shared water pump.

Houses are built back-to-back and in rows with no gardens.

Toilets in outhouses

Workhouses

People who had no money, or couldn't work, were sent to live in places called workhouses, which were almost like prisons. Once in the workhouses, they had to work very long hours and it was hard to get out again. Living conditions were harsh. Families were split up and hardly ever allowed to see each other. New inmates had to give up their own clothes and wear uniforms which branded them as paupers. The food was pretty limited, too: there was a fixed menu of potatoes, bread, cheese and soup, served in small portions that often left people still hungry.

Charity

Workhouses were the last resort of the very poorest people. Other Victorians living in poverty had to rely on charity. Churches and organizations such as the Salvation Army and Dr. Barnado's ran soup kitchens and shelters for the needy. They also campaigned to improve the lives of the poor, for better living conditions and fairer wages.

Many parents were so poor that they couldn't afford to look after their children. Dr. Barnardo's charity took care of homeless children like these and gave them shelter and education.

Shopping

The busy city streets provided many with a source of money. Working-class women and children often supplemented their family's incomes by selling flowers, fruit or matches on street corners. Many Victorian shopkeepers prospered and moved out of the cities to the suburbs, becoming part of the growing middle class. A number of modern British department stores began as market stalls and small shops that expanded to meet the Victorians' growing demand for goods and services.

Did you know? Poor city children were often forced to scavenge. "Toshers" searched in the sewers for anything they could sell, while "mudlarks" combed the riverbanks at low tide.

Crime and punishment

Law and order was a hot topic in Victorian society. As the towns and cities swelled, crime rates also soared at an alarming rate. Sensational accounts of crimes were regularly published in the popular press, which also raised people's fears. The Victorian solutions were police and prisons.

On the beat

Britain didn't have a permanent, government-run police force until Victoria's reign. In 1829, a politician named Robert Peel had established the Metropolitan police, but only in London. The police force was gradually extended and by 1856 the whole country was policed. The police soon became known as "bobbies" after Robert Peel. The main aim of the bobbies on the beat was to patrol the streets, to prevent crime and protect people and their property, but other duties included lighting street lamps and calling out the time.

Punishment

It didn't take much to get put in prison in Victorian times. Police records show that children as young as eight were jailed for crimes as petty as stealing a loaf of bread. Over 200 crimes carried the death penalty and other punishments included flogging and transportation. Thousands of convicts were bundled onto ships and transported to penal colonies in Australia, where they worked on farms and in heavy construction.

This 1830s cartoon shows a policeman who has apprehended a youth found loitering suspiciously.

Early policemen, like this one, wore a tail coat and reinforced top hat, because Peel didn't want them to look like a military force. In 1860, the uniform changed to a tunic and helmet more like those worn by the police today.

Internet links

For a link to a website where you can play the part of a Victorian bobby and find out why the prisons were so tough on criminals, go to **www.usborne-quicklinks.com**

12

Behind bars

The Victorians generally believed that the purpose of prisons was punishment, rather than rehabilitation. So they designed the prison experience to be as unpleasant as possible, to deter people from committing crimes. In some prisons, inmates had to keep silent at all times and were forced to wear masks to prevent them from communicating with one another. They were given deliberately dreary, repetitive work, including unpicking old ropes to be made into string and walking 2,400m (8,000ft) on a treadwheel for eight hours a day. It is hardly surprising that some prisoners went insane.

This Victorian painting shows convicts trudging around in circles in a prison exercise yard.

This illustration from Conan Doyle's story *The Naval Treaty*, shows Sherlock Holmes examining evidence in his chemistry laboratory as Dr. Watson looks on.

Notorious crimes

The introduction of police led to a substantial drop in crime, but a number of particularly gruesome, high-profile crimes still hit the headlines. One of the most infamous cases was of a serial killer in London's East End in the 1880s. The murderer became known as Jack the Ripper, but his true identity was never discovered. Partly because the case was never solved, he has been the subject of horror novels, gory music hall shows and movies ever since.

Detective work

The detective arm of the police force was formed in 1842. The "Jack the Ripper" case was one of the first in which they used forensic, or scientific, evidence. These new methods helped to make policing and the criminal justice system more effective. Forensic science was also made popular with the publication of stories by Arthur Conan Doyle about a fictional detective named Sherlock Holmes.

Did you know? Until they were abolished in 1868, public executions, held in the streets, drew huge crowds. Some people even paid large sums to rent rooms with a good view.

At school

At the start of Victoria's reign, around two-thirds of the population was illiterate. All education cost money, which most parents couldn't afford, so many children went without. For the children who did go to school, the sort of education they were given varied a lot, depending on whether they were rich or poor, boys or girls. But, over the years, the government began to take more responsibility for education. By the end of Victoria's reign, school was compulsory and free for all children up to 12 years old. The nation was now better educated than ever before.

"Dame" schools, like this one, provided only very basic education for the youngest children. They were often more like babysitting services than schools.

Elite education

Boys from wealthy families were mostly sent to exclusive private schools, where they learned Latin and Greek before going on to universities. Their sisters' schooling was usually far more limited. They were educated at home and taught subjects that were considered "womanly" – such as needlework and music.

Victorian children, like this boy, did their school work on slates, not on paper.

Education for all

For working class children, there were schools run by charities and churches, and "dame" schools, where unmarried women taught in their own homes. But even these schools charged a fee, which many couldn't afford. It wasn't until 1870 that the government provided education for everyone and had hundreds of new schools built.

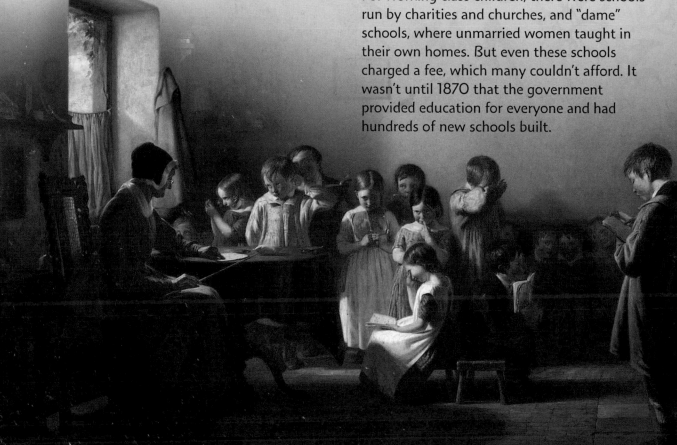

The "three Rs"

Lessons focussed on what the Victorians called the "three Rs" – Reading, wRiting and aRithmetic. A lot of lessons were dull, by today's standards. Pupils repeated what the teacher told them, again and again, until they knew it by heart. There were hardly any text books, so children copied lessons onto their slates, which were like mini blackboards that could be used again. Discipline was severe. Talking in class was forbidden and teachers often beat naughty or less able pupils.

Learning to do the laundry (as you can see in this photograph from 1893) was considered a vital part of education for Victorian girls.

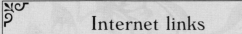
Internet links

For a link to a website where you can find out what it would be like to go to a Victorian school, go to **www.usborne-quicklinks.com**

Life lessons

Victorians thought education should equip children for adult life. To prepare them for work in trades, boys learned mathematics, woodwork and technical drawing in addition to the "three Rs" and traditional subjects such as history and geography. Girls weren't expected to need as much education as boys, so they were given lessons in cooking, sewing and housework. Usually, only private schoolboys, future professionals, continued at school after 12 years old.

Games

Victorians believed that healthy bodies made healthy minds. Boys at private schools, such as Rugby, Harrow and Eton, played sports including soccer, cricket and rugby. Most other schools had lessons known as drill, when pupils jogged on the spot, lifted weights and stretched in formation. At playtime and after school, children played their own games with balls, hoops, marbles and skipping ropes.

 Did you know? The game of rugby was reputedly invented during a soccer match at Rugby school in 1823, when a boy named William Webb Ellis caught a ball and ran with it.

15

Victoria and Albert

Victoria's German cousin Albert was regarded by her family as a suitable husband for her from early on. But when they first met at 17, the two cousins didn't get along. Victoria could be hot-headed and rash, while Albert was cool and rational. But four years later they were married. By then their differences brought out the best in each other and they grew to be a devoted couple.

The royal wedding

On October 15, 1839, Victoria asked Albert to marry her – it would have been improper for a prince to propose to the Queen – and he accepted. The following year, on February 10, hordes of waving, cheering Londoners crowded outside Buckingham Palace to catch a glimpse of their queen as her coach drove past. Most royal brides at the time wore silver gowns, but Victoria's dress was made of white satin and lace. In her hair, were diamonds and orange blossom, and over her heart she wore a diamond and sapphire brooch – a gift from Albert.

Prince Albert is painted here in fashionable formal dress.

An uncrowned king

Prince Albert was a quiet, clever man. Although he was happy for Victoria to take the limelight, he was frustrated that he had no official title or duty. At first, his only job was to blot Victoria's signature on official papers. Gradually, Victoria relied more and more on his help and advice, until they were effectively ruling together. But parliament refused to make Albert king. So in 1857 Victoria gave him the title of Prince Consort, in recognition of his importance to her and to the country.

Queen Victoria and her family posed for this informal portrait at Osborne House, on the Isle of Wight.

Country living

Victoria and Albert adored their nine children. Most of the year, they lived in Windsor Castle, but they also had two country homes. Osborne House, on the Isle of Wight, and Balmoral Castle, in Scotland, gave them an escape from the formality of public life. There, the couple worked in the mornings and spent the rest of the day with their children. They enjoyed simple pastimes such as walking, riding and painting. Many Victorians saw them as the ideal happy family.

The Widow of Windsor

Tragically, in 1861, Prince Albert was diagnosed with typhoid and died soon after, at just 42. Victoria was heartbroken. She spent the next ten years in inconsolable mourning, away from the public. The prime minister, Benjamin Disraeli, eventually persuaded her to return to public life, but the Queen wore black for the rest of her life.

John Brown

John Brown was a servant in charge of the stables at Balmoral. At the height of Victoria's grief, her doctor suggested that exercise might help, so he invited Brown to Windsor to take the Queen out riding. Victoria formed a close friendship with him, because he reminded her of Albert. But it caused a scandal among many people, who thought that a servant shouldn't be so familiar with the Queen. Some gossips even hinted that they had married in secret.

This painting shows John Brown taking Victoria out on her horse.

 Did you know? Victoria outlived Albert by 40 years, but never accepted his death. She insisted that servants put out fresh clothes for him every day.

17

In the home

Home life improved dramatically for the new middle classes in Victoria's reign. Mass-production gave people a greater choice of home furnishings and household goods, and at lower prices. Better transportation also increased the range of foods available in the shops, and new technology allowed gas and water to be piped into people's houses, providing better lighting and sanitation.

Masters and servants

Most middle-class homes employed at least one servant. Even the least well-off had a maid, who visited the house daily to help with the housework. Richer families might employ a butler to answer the door and wait on the family, a cook, footmen to serve food and numerous maids to help cook, serve food and clean.

Mrs. Beeton

Every Victorian housewife tried to run her home efficiently and economically, and there were plenty of books offering advice on the best way to do this. One of the most famous was Mrs. Beeton's *Book of Household Management*, which included advice on how to furnish a house, how to save money, what to do in medical emergencies, as well as over two thousand recipes.

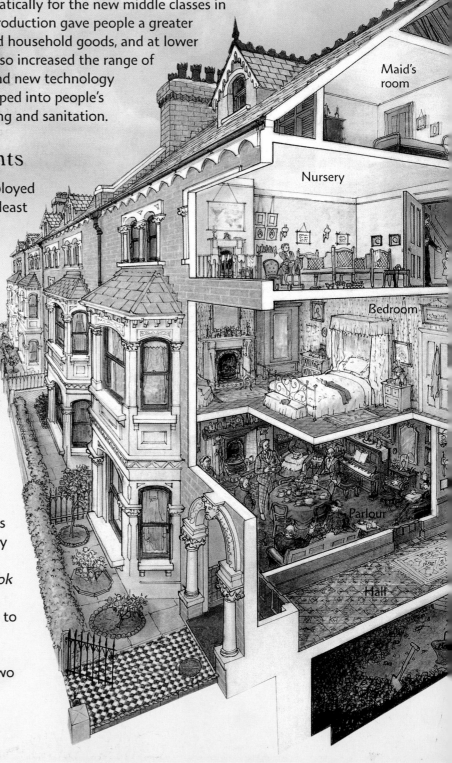

Maid's room

Nursery

Bedroom

Parlour

Hall

This is a Victorian family house in around 1880, cut away so you can see inside.

Servants' quarters were usually tucked away in the attic, as separate from the rest of the household as possible.

Canned and packaged foods first appeared in Victorian times. Many thought they were safer and healthier than fresh foods.

Food and drink

The Victorian diet was very stodgy by today's standards. People ate lots of potatoes and bread, but little fresh fruit or vegetables. Meat was central to most menus, including cuts that are less common today, such as bull's heart, sheep's head, pig's face or calf's head (including the eyes, tongue and brain). No dinner was complete without a pudding. Many people also ate afternoon tea – sandwiches and cakes, served with tea.

Toilet

Laundry

Scullery for washing-up

Kitchen

Internet links

For a link to a website where you can take a virtual tour of a Victorian house, go to **www.usborne-quicklinks.com**

Cleaning up

Keeping things spotless wasn't easy without vacuum cleaners and washing machines. All housework had to be done by hand, so it took much longer than it does now. Entire days were devoted just to doing the laundry or the baking, and housewives used all sorts of tricks to make things appear as clean as possible, even if they were really quite dirty. They used a blue dye to make "white" laundry look whiter, and rubbed black lead on their stoves to make them look new.

Cellar

The front room on the ground floor of the house was known as the parlour. This room would contain all the best furnishings and was used for special occasions and receiving guests.

 Did you know? People often sprinkled carpets with damp tea-leaves or freshly cut grass before they swept them, to stop dust from flying all over the room.

Victorian women

In Victorian times, most people thought that a woman's place was in the home, whatever her class. Women were expected to get married and have children; those who failed to do this tended to be looked down upon or pitied.

Making ends meet

But for many the reality was different. Most working-class women had to take on paid work outside the home. The most common occupation was as a domestic servant. The hours were long, the pay was next-to-nothing and servants were given very little time off. But the alternative was often a life of extreme poverty. The second biggest employers of working-class women were factories who often paid the women far less than their male counterparts.

Womanly professions

Most middle-class women only went out to work if they had no husband or parents to support them. Suitable jobs included being a nanny or a teacher. These jobs weren't well paid, but most alternatives were not considered appropriate. Gradually, attitudes began to change. Florence Nightingale made nursing a more respectable career for women, and in 1865 Elizabeth Garrett Anderson became the first British woman to qualify as a doctor. But women like them were still very much in the minority and faced much opposition.

This woman is operating a weaving machine in a cotton mill. The conditions in these mills were often extremely cramped, as factory owners tried to fit as many machines as possible into the space.

Did you know? In 1867, as a result of a clerical error, a shopkeeper from Manchester named Lily Maxwell became the first woman to vote in an election.

Women's rights

Women were in many ways second-class citizens. They were often treated as their husband's or parents' property. At the beginning of Victoria's reign, women couldn't vote or go to universities and, when they married, all their possessions became their husband's.

Elizabeth Garrett Anderson, an active campaigner for women's rights

By the 1870s, some progress had been made. Women could now be awarded degrees at some universities and had a right to keep their own earnings. In the 1860s, several women's groups began campaigning for the right to vote in elections. In 1887 the suffragettes, as they were known, joined forces to form a powerful national union led by Millicent Fawcett, Lydia Becker and Emmeline Pankhurst. But it wasn't until 1928 that they achieved their goal.

Internet links

For a link to a website where you can play a game to find out how women's rights changed during Victoria's reign, go to **www.usborne-quicklinks.com**

Women's wear

Victorian women's clothing was often very uncomfortable. Dresses were designed to emphasize the hips and to make the waist look as tiny as possible. To achieve this, women wore very tightly laced bodices, called corsets, under their dresses. Corsets severely restricted how women moved and sat – and even how much they could eat. Skirts were worn over hooped frames, called crinolines, which were designed to make them look as full as possible. Compared to corsets these were comfortable, but they sometimes made sitting or walking through doorways difficult.

As this extraordinary photograph shows, getting dressed could be quite a feat for a fashionable Victorian woman.

Politics and power

Until the 19th century, the British political system hadn't changed for centuries. The only people who could stand for parliament or vote in elections were aristocratic landowners who paid little attention to the lives of ordinary people. Then, in 1832, came the first of many reform acts which made elections more democratic and gradually extended the vote to more and more men. But women still had to wait until the 20th century.

This illustration shows Queen Victoria with Benjamin Disraeli – the prime minister she liked best.

Party politics

Two political parties dominated parliament for most of Victoria's reign: the Liberals who supported political reform, and the Conservatives, or Tories, who were usually against change. As more working people gained the vote, the old system was shaken up with the emergence of a third party, which eventually became the Labour party.

The Houses of Parliament were designed by Charles Barry after the original buildings were destroyed in a fire in 1834. Queen Victoria opened the new parliament buildings in 1852.

Victoria's ministers

By Victorian times, Britain was a constitutional monarchy, which meant that political power rested with the government, not with the Queen. But Victoria still held some influence, so ministers had to try to get along with her. Ten prime ministers held office during her reign. Two of the most prominent were the Conservative Benjamin Disraeli, whose smooth talk and flattery won her respect, and his less sympathetic Liberal rival, William Gladstone, who Queen Victoria disliked intensely.

Protest and petitions

At the beginning of Victoria's reign, fewer than one in seven men could vote. In 1838, a group of workers published a people's charter demanding more reforms. These included the right for every man to vote in secret, and salaries for members of parliament so that anyone could afford to enter politics. In 1848, the Chartists, as they became known, sent a petition containing over five million signatures to parliament. It was rejected at first, but eventually the government met many of the Chartist's demands.

Revolutions and reforms

In 1848 a wave of revolutions swept across Europe, as many people turned against their rulers. In the same year, German political thinkers Karl Marx and Friedrich Engels published *The Communist Manifesto*, which called for workers to rise against their employers to create a classless society. But the revolution didn't hit Britain, where most reformers preferred to change things legally from inside the system. By the 1880s, as a result of pressure put on the government, most working men had been given the vote.

This illustration shows the Matchgirls' Union strike of 1871, when over 1,400 match factory workers protested against dangerous working conditions.

United front

In the 1830s and 40s, working people started to form groups called trade unions. The unions challenged employers and the government, demanding better pay, shorter hours and safer places to work. When union members wanted to protest about something, they all agreed to stop working and go on strike. In 1892, a former mining union leader named James Kier Hardie became the first working-class member of parliament. A year later, he set up the Independent Labour Party, which later developed into the modern Labour Party. At last, working people had a political party that could represent them in parliament.

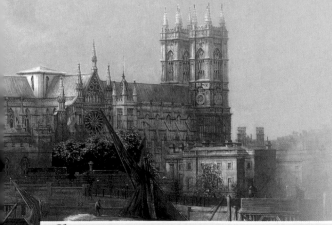

Internet links

For a link to a website where you can read more about Disraeli, Gladstone and other Victorian prime ministers, go to
www.usborne-quicklinks.com

 Did you know? Victorian politicians wore long coats and top hats to Parliament. Kier Hardie caused an uproar when he turned up in his working-class outfit of a cloth cap and tweed suit.

23

Building an empire

I n 1877, Victoria acquired an exotic new title: Empress of India. By the end of her reign in 1901, vast areas of the map of the world – from the wheatfields of Canada and the sugar plantations of the Caribbean, to the jungles and deserts of India and Africa – were painted red or pink, symbolizing British rule. The British empire became known as the "empire on which the sun never set" because it was the largest the world had ever known and was home to nearly a quarter of the world's population.

The pink areas on this world map show the extent of the British empire in 1886.

Traders and settlers

The empire developed from colonies overseas where for centuries people had gone to trade or settle and make a new life. Since the 1600s, a British trading company called the East India Company had held a number of ports and settlements in India under its control. As the Indian Mogul empire became weaker and weaker, the Company took over more and more land. By Victoria's reign, large parts of India were technically in British hands. But the idea of an empire still wasn't very strong in people's minds.

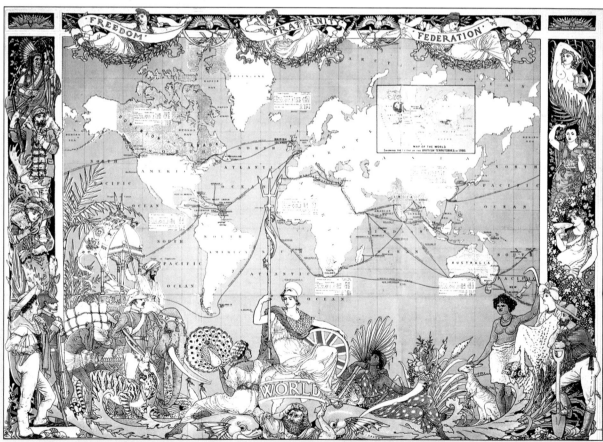

Did you know? Tea became a popular everyday drink in Victorian times, when it was imported in bulk from China, India and Sri Lanka. Until then it was a luxury only available to wealthy people.

The Indian mutiny

Then, in 1856, something happened to change things dramatically. A story spread that Indian soldiers in the British Army had been issued with rifle cartridges smeared with cow and pig fat, which offended their religious sensitivities. The soldiers mutinied and protest spread across northern India. The mutiny lasted 13 months, and thousands died.

One of Victoria's Indian subjects

The "Jewel in the Crown"

A year later, the British government decided the only solution was to take direct control of India, which now became the keystone of the empire, and the focus for rivalry with other European countries. Rail networks were built, industries developed, and trade expanded. India became a great source of wealth and prosperity. In 1877, Disraeli persuaded Victoria to take the title "Empress of India" and he described India as the "jewel" in her crown.

The Scramble for Africa

In the second half of Victoria's reign, European nations competed for land in Africa. There was a demand for new sources of raw materials for industry, and Africa was seen as the last great unexplored wilderness. Soon railways were built, opening up new regions for trade and exploiting the rich supplies of gold, diamonds and other minerals. By 1914, most of Africa was in European control. It became known as the "Scramble for Africa" because it all happened so fast.

But it wasn't all about trade and politics. Many other Victorians went there to explore, or as missionaries, to convert people to Christianity, setting up schools and hospitals. This may seem arrogant to us now, but most missionaries believed they were doing good.

Internet links

For a link to a website with maps, timelines and Victorian paintings of the British empire, go to **www.usborne-quicklinks.com**

Lord Curzon, seated in the middle, was Governor General and Viceroy of India in 1899-1904. Hunting tigers was a popular sport of princes in India, and the English rulers were no exception.

Great exhibitions

The Great Exhibition of 1851 was one of the highlights of the Victorian age. It was masterminded by Prince Albert and Henry Cole, a civil servant, as a celebration of the industrial age and Britain's leading role in it. The enormous show of arts, produce and manufactured goods attracted visitors and exhibitors from all around the world and won Albert the admiration of his subjects.

Visitors to the newly-opened Natural History Museum admiring exotic stuffed animals

A palace for a new age

The exhibition was housed in Crystal Palace, a gigantic structure of glass and steel, put up specially in Hyde Park, in London. It was designed by Joseph Paxton, a former gardener who based it on a much smaller greenhouse he had built for the Duke of Devonshire. The building itself was a spectacular tribute to British engineering and design. Not only was it the first building of its kind, but it was colossal – covering an area the size of four soccer fields.

On show

Queen Victoria opened the Great Exhibition on May 1, 1851. For the next six months, millions of people visited London to see it. Among the rare and exotic things on show were furs from Russia, an entire Turkish bazaar and a Tunisian nomads' tent covered in lion skins. But what excited people most was the machine hall. This housed an awesome display of new technology – from printing presses and threshing machines to powerful locomotive engines. The Crystal Palace was like a crystal ball, offering its visitors a vision of the wider world and of the future.

This painting shows the front entrance of Crystal Palace. The flags along the roof show all the nations that took part in the exhibition.

Great numbers

- 300,000 panes of hand-blown glass were used to build the Crystal Palace, which comprised nearly a million square feet of floor space and was tall enough to accommodate two giant elms that were growing on the site.
- 2,700 men were employed to build the Crystal Palace in just six months.
- 13,000 exhibits were shown.
- 6,000,000 people visited the Great Exhibition.
- 750,000 visitors came to Crystal Palace by train.
- 250,000 people bought season tickets so they could visit several times.
- The entry fee was 5 shillings at first. After three weeks Prince Albert brought in cheaper tickets. On the first "shilling day" 37,000 people turned up.
- Queen Victoria and her family visited the exhibition 13 times.

The inside of the central transept, shown here, was the tallest part of Crystal Palace. During the ceremony it was filled with the voices of three cathedral choirs singing Handel's *Messiah*.

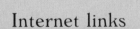

Internet links

For a link to a website where you can see a Virtual Reality model of Crystal Palace, go to **www.usborne-quicklinks.com**

After the exhibition, the Crystal Palace was taken down and rebuilt in the London suburb of Sydenham, where it stood until it was destroyed by a fire in 1936.

Albert's legacy

The Great Exhibition ended in October 1851, having made a massive profit. Prince Albert invested the money in art and science education by setting up the Royal Colleges of Music and Art, the Imperial College of Science and several museums. These included the Natural History Museum, the Science Museum and the Museum of Ornamental Art (now called the Victoria and Albert Museum). The museums were free, so everyone could enjoy them. After the success of the Great Exhibition, people became very enthusiastic about visiting exhibitions. Soon, museums and art galleries sprang up in towns all around Britain.

Did you know? One of the more bizarre objects on display at the exhibition was an alarmed bed that could be set to hurl the sleeper straight into a cold bath in the morning.

Invention and discovery

Many inventions and discoveries that we take for granted today had their origins in Victorian times. Some of these discoveries had practical benefits, while others revolutionized the way people thought about themselves and their place in the world.

Ada Lady Lovelace, the world's first computer programmer

Electrical energy

People had known about electricity for hundreds of years, but in the 1830s scientist Michael Faraday invented a reliable way of generating an electric current. He found that when he moved a magnet in and out of a wire coil, the wire became charged with electricity. This was the first ever dynamo. This discovery was crucial to many of the electrical innovations that followed.

Bright lights

In 1878 and 1879, Joseph Swan in Britain and Thomas Edison in America both independently invented electric lightbulbs and people began to replace their smelly, smoky gas lamps with clean, bright, electric lights. The Houses of Parliament were soon lit with electric lightbulbs and Queen Victoria had them installed in all her palaces.

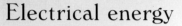

This is one of Joseph Swan's earliest lightbulbs from 1878.

Early computers

People think of computers as being a recent invention, but a Victorian mathematician named Charles Babbage designed a machine that was in many ways like a modern computer. He claimed that his "analytical engine" could carry out complex calculations automatically. His machine used simple programs, but worked without microchips or electricity. The programs were written by Ada Lovelace, daughter of the famous poet Lord Byron. Sadly, Babbage ran out of money before he could build his machine.

Monsters from the past

For centuries, people had been digging up mysterious giant bones, but no one knew what they were. By the 1820s, most scientists realized they must be the fossilized remains of huge reptiles that lived millions of years ago. In 1842, scientist Richard Owen studied these fossils and found that they belonged to a group that was quite distinct from reptiles. He named them dinosaurs, which means "terrible lizard" in Greek.

Did you know? A hundred years after his death, a working model of Babbage's machine was finally built, following his original designs. It is now on display in the Science Museum, in London.

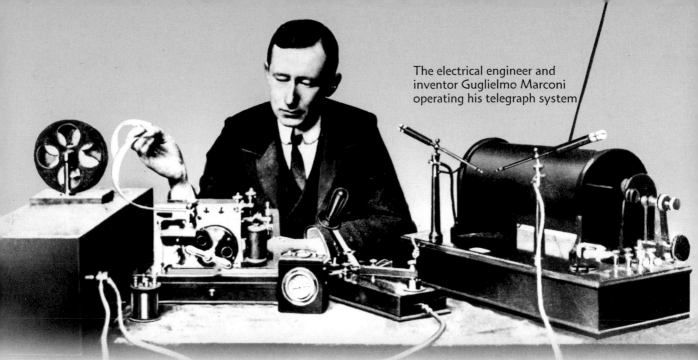
The electrical engineer and inventor Guglielmo Marconi operating his telegraph system

Hanging on the wire

New systems of global communication transformed the way the Victorians ran businesses, fought wars and broadcast news. The first electric telegraph machine – which sent instant messages, or telegrams, by passing electrical signals along a wire cable – was introduced in 1837. In 1875, Alexander Graham Bell, a Scottish man living in America, took things even further by inventing the telephone, to send speech along electrical wires. Then, in 1898, an Italian scientist, Guglielmo Marconi, set up his Wireless Telegraph Company in London, sending messages along radio waves.

Internet links

For a link to a website where you can see an animated description of Darwin's theory of evolution, go to
www.usborne-quicklinks.com

This Victorian cartoon of Charles Darwin pokes fun at his theory that people had evolved from apes.

The theory of evolution

In 1859, the English scientist Charles Darwin published his radical theory of evolution suggesting that species of plants and animals had developed, or evolved, over the centuries. This allowed them to adapt as the environment changed, so that the species that adapted best, survived and passed on their characteristics to their offspring. Most people believed that God had created all living things at the same time and so many were outraged at Darwin's theory. But his ideas now form the basis of much modern thinking about the natural sciences.

On the move

For many people in Britain, the world became a smaller place in Victorian times. Until then, most had never been further than the next town. But that all changed, as the Victorians built up a vast integrated network of local and national train lines, with connecting bus and tram services, making travel quicker, easier and cheaper than ever before.

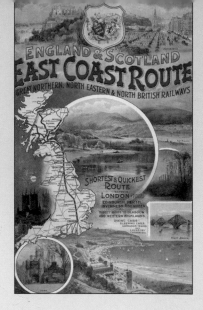

This Victorian railway poster, advertizes the route between England and Scotland. The map shows how the rail network extends across the country.

Railway mania

The first passenger train was launched in 1825, but it wasn't until the 1840s that passenger travel really took off. Rail travel became popular with everyone and the railways grew at an astonishing rate. To meet the growing demand, train companies and travel agents sprang up, offering excursions to the seaside, to exhibitions and even to public executions. Between 1845 and 1900, the number of passengers on Britain's railways tripled.

In 1863, the world's first underground railway opened in London. At first, passengers sat in open wagons pulled by steam locomotives. Imagine being covered in soot in the smoky, narrow tunnels! Things improved a lot with the introduction of cleaner, electric underground trains in 1890. Rail travel above ground also became more comfortable, as dining cars, sleeping carriages and lavatories were introduced on trains.

This photograph from 1892 shows an *Iron Duke* steam train pulling out of Paddington station, in London.

Did you know? Queen Victoria made her first train trip in 1842. After that, she made frequent journeys by rail in a specially-built, plush royal carriage.

Standard time

It's hard to imagine now, but people around the country used to set their watches to different times, depending on where they lived. For example, Oxford was 5 minutes behind London. This caused chaos with train timetables – people missed connections and trains from rail companies using different local times could arrive at the same platform at the same time. Gradually, rail companies all changed to London time and in 1880 it was finally adopted by the whole country, by law.

This photograph shows a double-decker horse-drawn bus, covered in advertizing posters. The first double-decker buses were introduced in 1847. Passengers on the top deck paid half fares.

Horse power

By comparison with the railways, travel by road developed at a much slower pace. Most urban buses and trams (buses that run on tracks set into the roads) were pulled by horses until the 1890s. Then, buses became motorized for the first time and trams switched to electricity.

Horseless carriages

The earliest cars, known as horseless carriages, appeared in around 1885. But they were mostly imported from Germany and France, at a price most people could only dream of. At first, cars were forced to drive extremely slowly, because of the Red Flag Act of 1865. This required all self-powered road vehicles to be driven behind a man walking with a red flag. The law was lifted in 1896, but it wasn't until cars began to be mass-produced in the early 20th century that people enthusiastically took up the idea of travel by car.

Internet links

For a link to a website where you can play a game to find out how an early steam locomotive worked, go to **www.usborne-quicklinks.com**

Victorians at war

Victoria's reign was a time of relative peace in Europe. But, as European countries competed for colonies in far-flung corners of the world, it led to clashes between them, as well as resistance from local people. These sometimes developed into full-scale wars.

The Crimean War

One of the bloodiest, most disorganized wars in European history took place in the Crimea, a region by the Black Sea between Russia and Turkey, in 1854-1856. It began as a dispute between Russia and the Ottoman Turks, but soon involved France and Britain, who wanted to limit Russia's power in the area.

The war was notorious for the huge numbers of soldiers who died on both sides: as many as half the 1,200,000 who were sent to fight lost their lives. Many were killed in battle, often because of the incompetence of their officers. But even more died of diseases such as cholera, infected wounds, and from extreme cold and starvation. One thing was entirely new: this was the first war ever to have journalists on the spot, filing reports. At breakfast back in London, people could read the shocking horrors of the war in their daily copies of *The Times*.

Below is a scene from *The Charge of the Light Brigade*, a movie made in 1936, about one of the most disastrous battles of the Crimean War.

African resistance

In many parts of Africa, the British established colonies relatively easily. But they met their match in two areas where resistance was strong – against the Zulus of southern Africa, and the Muslim kingdoms of Sudan to the north.

With the Zulus, Britain came up against a fierce, disciplined warrior nation. Armed only with spears and shields, the Zulus inflicted a crushing victory on the better-equipped British soldiers at the Battle of Isandhwana in 1879. Still reeling from the shock, the British faced another blow in 1884-85, when a religious leader known as the Mahdi led an uprising against them in Sudan. The rebels killed the British commander, General Gordon, and held out for several years. Sudan finally came under Anglo-Egyptian control in 1899.

General Gordon

Boer fighters, like these two sitting on top of a cannon, weren't professional soldiers, but they fought hard for their country.

The Anglo-Boer Wars

By the 1870s, the British controlled two colonies in South Africa, the Cape and Natal, while the Boers (Dutch settlers) had two republics, Transvaal and Orange Free State. Relations between them broke down when Britain took over the Transvaal in 1877. The Boers rebelled and after the first war, 1880-1881, they won back Transvaal's independence.

But the discovery of gold there in 1886 meant there was now much more at stake. Clashes between Boers and the English-speaking workers brought in to mine the gold led to a second bitter war. The Boers adopted guerilla tactics, sending small units of men to capture supplies and attack when least expected. In response, the British burned down their farms and imprisoned their families in prison camps, where thousands died of disease. The war finally ended with a British victory in 1902.

Internet links

For a link to a website where you can find out more about the history of the British Army, go to **www.usborne-quicklinks.com**

Did you know? After visiting the wounded in the hospital after the Crimean War, Queen Victoria was appalled by the suffering she saw, and introduced a medal for gallantry: the Victoria Cross.

33

Troubles in Ireland

Relations between Britain and Ireland had been uneasy for centuries. But, since 1801, Ireland had been part of the United Kingdom, ruled by the British government in London. While a few Irish people prospered under British rule, most lived as farmers in dreadful poverty and many held their foreign rulers to blame.

Landlords and agents

Most of Ireland's farmland was owned by aristocrats who lived in England and employed agents to manage their estates for them. The agents then leased the land to local farmers for a profit. The more tenants they had, the more rent they collected, so the land was divided into the smallest farms possible.

The potato famine

Most Irish peasant farmers had only enough land to grow what they needed to survive. Potatoes were the staple diet and many had almost no other crops to fall back on. If there was a bad harvest, and they were unable to pay their rent, agents often had them evicted.

Disaster struck in 1845, when the potato crop became infected with a fungal disease, called blight, which turned the potatoes to an inedible black pulp. The next two years also saw failed harvests. By 1850, over a million people had died and a further two million had emigrated, mostly to America, in search of a better life. Unable to pay their rent, thousands more were evicted, left starving and homeless.

The Victorian Irish family in this picture were forced to live in this hut after being evicted from their farm for failing to pay their rent.

Irish anger

After the famine, many Irish people felt that the government could have done more to help and that things might have been better if they ruled themselves. With financial help from angry Irish settlers in America, a number of secret organizations were formed, to fight for independence from Britain. Their members called themselves Fenians and some of their campaigns led to violence, at home and in England, as they fought for their cause.

This engraving from 1865 shows Irish emigrants preparing to set sail for a new life in America.

Charles Stuart Parnell

One man working for independence, or Home Rule, by peaceful means was the brilliant Irish politician Charles Stuart Parnell. He aimed to improve the lives of Irish farmers, calling for fairer rents and the sale of land so that they could eventually buy their own farms. By 1885, his party had 86 members of parliament in London and he worked to bring attention to Ireland's cause by being as disruptive in parliament as possible. But in 1889 Parnell was involved in a divorce scandal. He left office in disgrace, his party split and the Home Rule cause was weakened without him.

Gladstone and Home Rule

The Liberal Prime Minister, William Gladstone, was determined to make peace in Ireland, and was convinced by Parnell that Home Rule was the way. In 1886 he tried to pass an Irish Home Rule Bill, but faced opposition from his own party and the Conservatives, who thought that it might lead to the break-up of the British empire. In 1893, he tried again, this time with the backing of the House of Commons, but he was narrowly defeated by the House of Lords. Gladstone retired the next year and the Irish problems remained unresolved.

Here Gladstone is defending Ireland against his opponent, Lord Salisbury.

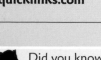

Internet links

For a link to a website where you can read more about modern Irish history, go to **www.usborne-quicklinks.com**

Did you know? Ireland achieved independence in 1921. But the country was divided into two and Ulster, in the North, remained in the United Kingdom, as it is today.

Health and medicine

By the mid-19th century, half of Britain's population lived in towns, many of them crowded into filthy, disease-ridden slums, where life expectancy could be as low as 29 years. As doctors didn't know what caused many diseases, or how they spread, hundreds of thousands died. During Victoria's reign, medical advances and improved living conditions led to lower death rates and greater life expectancy.

This cartoon shows a microscopic view of water from the River Thames, which is described as "Monster Soup" by the artist, George Cruikshank.

Deadly diseases

In the first four years of Victoria's reign 42,000 people died from smallpox, 50,000 died from measles and 64,000 caught typhoid. Most Victorians believed that these diseases were caused by foul-smelling air, known as miasma. Cholera was probably the most dreaded disease of all. In 1848 alone it killed 50,000 people. Cholera struck suddenly, causing dysentery, retching and extreme thirst, followed by pain in the limbs and stomach. When the patient's skin began to turn blue, it usually meant that they didn't have much time left to live.

In 1856, a doctor named John Snow proved that cholera was carried, not in the air, but in water polluted with sewage. He felt that better public sanitation could do much to prevent disease. Gradually, the government began to take responsibility for public health, building new sewerage systems, improving water supplies and ensuring that local councils collected household waste regularly.

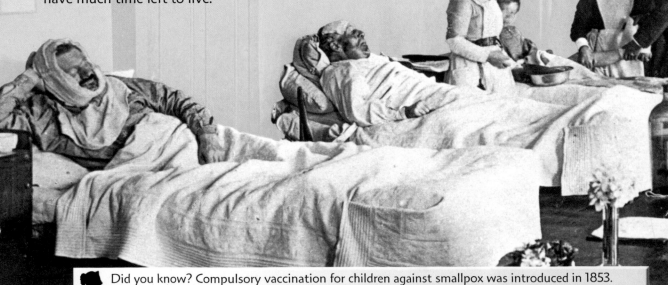

Did you know? Compulsory vaccination for children against smallpox was introduced in 1853. After that, the number of cases plummeted and the disease is unknown in Europe today.

Raising standards

Going to a hospital in Victorian times could be a risky business. Until the 1840s, surgeons didn't use anaesthetics to put people to sleep, or powerful pain killers to help with pain. So patients often died of shock during or after an operation. Doctors didn't clean their hands or instruments in between operations or examining patients, so fatal infections often spread. But the situation improved radically with the introduction of safe anaesthetics – chloroform gas in 1847 – and later, antiseptics. In 1869, a doctor named Joseph Lister invented an antiseptic spray to kill bacteria.

Internet links

For a link to a website where you can find out more about Florence Nightingale's life and her achievements, go to
www.usborne-quicklinks.com

To many Victorians, including the Queen herself, Florence Nightingale was a powerful symbol of feminine virtue.

This photograph was taken in a ward in the Royal Infirmary in Aberdeen in 1890. It's much cleaner than hospital wards were before Florence Nightingale's reforms.

Lady with the lamp

Florence Nightingale, sometimes known as the Lady with the Lamp, was an English nurse who fought hard for the improvement of conditions in hospitals. In 1854, during the Crimean War, she took a team of 38 nurses to Turkey to work in the army hospitals. Within weeks, they reduced the number of soldiers dying in hospitals from 42% to 2%. They did this mainly by improving hygiene. Nightingale became a nurse against the wishes of her family, but her work helped to make nursing a respectable career for women.

Books and the press

In the days before television or movies, books were a very important source of entertainment. As more and more people could read and write, the number of people reading for pleasure increased, creating demand for new, cheap forms of reading matter. The invention of steam-powered printing presses at the beginning of the 19th century meant that publishers were now able to print thousands of copies of books, papers or magazines at a time, to keep up with the unprecedented demand.

Internet links

For a link to a website where you can see some famous Victorian children's book illustrations, go to **www.usborne-quicklinks.com**

The Mad Hatter's tea party, from Lewis Carroll's *The Nursery Alice*, illustrated by John Tenniel

Children's books

In early Victorian times, people thought children's books should be educational, and include a moral for children to learn. After Lewis Carroll's *Alice's Adventures in Wonderland* was published in 1865, a whole new range of children's books was written purely for entertainment. Themes varied from exciting adventure stories set in distant countries, such as Robert Louis Stevenson's *Treasure Island* and Rudyard Kipling's *Jungle Book*, to the nonsense rhymes of Edward Lear. New printing techniques also meant that these books could be fully illustrated, giving rise to a new generation of successful children's book illustrators.

Social comment

One of the most popular Victorian authors was Charles Dickens. He was one of the first authors to describe the many injustices in society, and the lives of the very poor. Dickens's family had been imprisoned for debt when he was 12, forcing him to work in a boot blacking factory, and he wrote about these dreadful experiences in his novels. Most of his books were first published in serial form, with each part ending on a cliff-hanger, to make sure the readers came back for the next issue. He was also a talented public speaker, who drew huge audiences of eager fans to his public readings, both at home and in America.

This illustration from Charles Dickens's *Oliver Twist* shows the Artful Dodger teaching Oliver how to pick a gentleman's pocket.

Pulp fiction

The Victorians loved trashy stories just as much as people today. Cheaply produced paperback booklets, known as "penny dreadfuls" – including romance, adventure, mysteries and detective stories – were particularly popular. They came in weekly parts that cost just a penny, so almost anyone could afford them. But they were looked down on because the writing wasn't very good and their subjects were often rather sensational.

Read all about it

There had been newspapers in Britain since the late 18th century. But they were expensive, because paper was taxed, so not everyone could afford to buy them. When the tax was removed in 1855, papers began to circulate more widely. A new type of printing press, using rolls of paper instead of sheets, also made printing quicker and cheaper.

 Did you know? Many Victorian women authors – including Mary Ann Evans, who is better-known as George Eliot – took male pen names, because writing was considered unsuitable for women.

Time out

Until Victorian times, very few people could afford any time out for leisure activities. But by the second half of Victoria's reign, industry was booming and the country was more prosperous. The government introduced new public holidays and limited the number of hours people could be made to work. All this meant that, for the first time, many people had time to spend on having fun.

Seaside pleasures

The growth of rail travel in the 19th century, made it possible for working people to escape the grime of the cities cheaply and quickly, for a revitalizing trip to the seaside. As more and more people flocked to the beaches, Victorian seaside resorts grew rapidly. Hotels, piers, concert halls and shopping arcades sprang up to meet the increasing demand.

This cartoon shows a typical Victorian seaside scene. Many Victorians were very strict about the way they dressed. They went to the beach fully clothed and rented bathing huts, so they could change into their swimming costumes in private.

This photograph shows a Victorian lady riding an ordinary bicycle, sidesaddle.

Pedal power

Remarkably, bicycles were invented long after the steam train. The "ordinary bicycle" was the first design to catch on. It was difficult to mount and very unstable because the back wheel was smaller than the front one. In the 1880s, "safety bicycles" were invented. They were more like modern bikes, with wheels of equal size, gears and brakes. From then on, cycling was all the rage. During the weekends, parks and lanes were filled with eager cyclists, dressed in the latest cycling fashions.

Stage shows

Without television or radio to entertain them, many Victorians amused themselves by going to plays or concerts. Bandstands were built in parks for people to listen to string quartets or brass bands. The rich went to operas or classical concerts in plush, elegant playhouses and concert halls. For poorer people, there were music halls, where you could pay a penny to watch comedy shows, acrobats or cabaret acts.

This poster advertizes the Hackney Empire, one of Victorian London's most successful music halls.

Healthy competition

For hundreds of years, people had been playing many of the sports we play today, but without proper rules. Different versions of the same games were played in different parts of the country. This made competitions very unfair. Now people had more time to play sports, and could travel to compete, sports had to become more organized. Players formed organizations to enforce rules and set up local teams and large competitions. For the first time, watching sports became as big a pastime as playing them.

Sporting dates

- ✦ 1845 Boys at Rugby School first set the rules to their version of football – Rugby
- ✦ 1863 Football Association formed
- ✦ 1866 Amateur Athletic Club began
- ✦ 1871 Rugby Football Union set up
- ✦ 1872 First F.A. Cup competition held
- ✦ 1877 First international cricket Test Match
- ✦ 1877 First Wimbledon tennis championship
- ✦ 1888 Lawn Tennis Association established

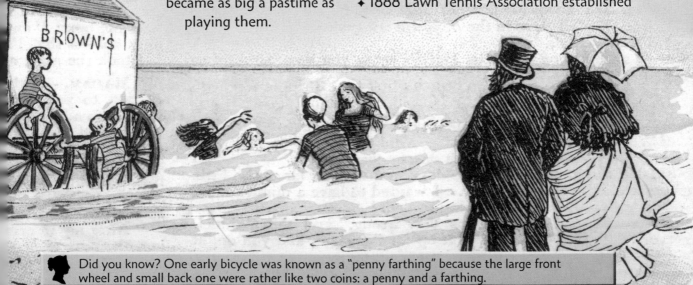

Did you know? One early bicycle was known as a "penny farthing" because the large front wheel and small back one were rather like two coins: a penny and a farthing.

Building and engineering

Many of the grandest, most ornate public buildings you can see in Britain today – town halls, railway stations, museums and schools – were built by the Victorians. They also laid thousands of miles of train tracks, canals and sewers, and constructed huge bridges and tunnels, changing the face of Britain forever. Many of these ambitious projects were made possible by the use of new building techniques and materials, such as steel and plate glass.

The Victorian Gothic style Royal Courts of Justice in London looks more like a cathedral than a law court.

Buildings with style

The Victorians were fascinated by the past, and this really shows in their architecture. The designs of several buildings were influenced by archaeological discoveries taking place in Europe at the time. Buildings like the British Museum in London were built in a Neo Classical style to look like the temples and arcades of Ancient Greece and Rome.

But they were probably even more inspired by the religion and romance of the Middle Ages. Many Victorian buildings, such as St. Pancras Station and the Houses of Parliament, were built in the style of medieval cathedrals. This style is known as Victorian Gothic and you can recognize it by its pointed arches, decorative carvings and high, vaulted ceilings.

Building bridges

One of the greatest engineers of the Victorian age was Isambard Kingdom Brunel, whose many achievements included bridges, steamships, docks and railway lines. His first big project was the Clifton Suspension Bridge, which crosses the Avon Gorge at Clifton, providing a vital link to the city of Bristol from the east. At 215m (700ft) long, it was the world's longest bridge at that time. While it was being built, Brunel also designed and oversaw the building of the Great Western Railway line between London and Bristol.

Brunel standing next to the giant landing chain of one of his vast steamships

Digging deep

Some of the most impressive Victorian construction and engineering work went on underground, where a vast network of sewers, underground train lines and tunnels was constructed. At first, these were usually built by a "cut and cover" method. This involved digging out a deep trench, building a roof and then covering it again. Later, new machinery made it possible to bore far deeper tunnels, without disrupting life up above. In the 1880s, British and French engineers used these machines to begin a tunnel under the English Channel, but it was abandonned for fear of a French invasion.

Internet links

For a link to a website where you can find out more about Brunel and his achievements, go to **www.usborne-quicklinks.com**

Brunel's Clifton Suspension Bridge was completed in 1864 and is still used today. Although the bridge was very modern for its time, Brunel designed the towers at each end in an Egyptian style.

Did you know? The massive Forth Railway Bridge, in Scotland, was completed in 1890. The building work took 54,000 tons of steel, 21,000 tons of cement and seven million rivets.

Victorian art

The changes taking place in Victorian society were reflected in changing tastes in art too. And the popularity of new museums and exhibitions meant that painting and sculpture reached a wider audience than ever before.

Realism and romance

In an age before soap opera, scenes from everyday life – especially ones that told a story – were immensely popular. Some artists painted the bustle of modern life, such as crowd scenes at train stations or a day at the races. But others showed sad scenes of sick children or people living in deep poverty. Today some people regard these paintings as sentimental, but they reflected real public concerns at the time. In painting, as in architecture, the Victorians were also inspired by the past and by exotic foreign cultures. They enjoyed romantic paintings of rushing torrents, windswept mountains and ghostly castles.

The Pre-Raphaelites

In 1848, a group of artists, including John Everett Millais, Dante Gabriel Rossetti and William Holman Hunt, formed a society, called the Pre-Raphaelite Brotherhood. They were influenced by art critic John Ruskin, who felt that industrial life was unspiritual and impersonal. Their idea was to return to the values of what they saw as a more religious time: the Middle Ages. The Pre-Raphaelites believed art should convey a moral message, and took many of their subjects from Shakespeare, the Bible and Arthurian legends. They painted from nature in fresh tones, with great attention to detail – rejecting art from the time of Renaissance artist Raphael as being too sophisticated and insincere.

Internet links

For a link to a website where you can find out more about the Pre-Raphaelite artists and their works, go to **www.usborne-quicklinks.com**

Ophelia, by John Everett Millais, illustrates the heroine's tragic death scene from *Hamlet*.

Still lives

The invention of photography also had an impact on art after the 1830s. One of the first and most influential art photographers was Julia Margaret Cameron, who took portraits of many leading Victorians. Photography also meant that works of art could be easily reproduced in popular magazines or as prints to be hung in people's homes.

Arts and crafts

William Morris, a member of the Pre-Raphaelite circle and a socialist, was concerned that in an age of machines the work of skilled craftsmen was no longer valued. He felt mass-production was leading to poor quality, and believed that even useful things should be hand-crafted, beautiful and unique. In the 1860s, Morris founded the Arts and Crafts movement. He and his followers used traditional crafts and medieval designs to produce wallpaper, pottery, textiles and furniture as well as paintings.

THE LADY OF THE LAKE TELLETH ARTHVR OF THE SWORD EXCALIBVR

Aubrey Beardsley's illustration shows King Arthur meeting the Lady of the Lake.

Art for art's sake

By the end of Victoria's reign another new style was emerging. As a reaction against the Victorian taste for moral messages, artists such as James Abbott McNeil Whistler, Aubrey Beardsley and Walter Crane believed that the only purpose of art was to be beautiful. These artists painted in a highly decorative style, influenced by Japanese art, French writers and artists and playwrights such as Oscar Wilde.

Popular classics

In the 18th century, classical themes – from Greek and Roman history and mythology, usually painted in a stiff, formal style – had appealed mainly to aristocratic patrons. But late Victorian artists, such as Alma Tadema, Albert Moore and Lord Leighton, revived these subjects in a more popular, romantic, decorative style, for a mass audience.

 Did you know? Millais was one of the most commercial Victorian artists. His painting *Bubbles* was reproduced on an advertisement for Pears soap, making him a very wealthy man.

The end of an era

On New Year's Day, 1900, people weren't sure whether it was the start of a new century, or the end of the old one. But, to many, January 22, 1901 was more significant still. That was the day Victoria died and the Victorian era came to an end. Many looked back over her reign, amazed at the progress that had been made, but they also looked forward to the new century with trepidation.

An uncertain future

Despite great progress in health and education, a third of the population were still very poor. The country was at war in Africa and violence in Ireland was escalating. Britain had led the world into the Industrial Revolution, but now the United States and Germany were begining to dominate the world market. Britain no longer had the power and influence it once held.

A celebrated life

Queen Victoria's popularity soared during her last years. Her golden and diamond jubilees marked 50 and 60 years on the throne with grand parades and street parties all over the country. Her funeral procession was grander still. London's streets were packed with mourners from every corner of the empire. Victoria, who had spent her last 40 years in widow's black, ordered a white funeral. The coffin was decked in white flowers, as it was taken to Windsor to be buried beside her beloved Albert.

In with the new

Victoria's eldest son, Edward Albert, the Prince of Wales, succeeded her to the throne. "Bertie" was a very different character from his mother. The Queen had considered him frivolous and irresponsible, and had refused to involve him in royal matters. Edward was 59 when he became king and he had a lot to live up to. But he became a popular, energetic monarch and people liked his relaxed, modern style of kingship.

Here you can see four generations of British monarchs: Victoria, her son Edward VII (right), her grandson George V (left) and her great-grandson Edward VIII.

Did you know? The future Edward VII enjoyed a life of gambling and excess. He became known as "Edward the wide" because of his great appetite for rich foods and fine wines.

Acknowledgements

Every effort has been made to trace the copyright holders of material in this book. If any rights have been omitted, the publishers offer their sincere apologies and will rectify this in any subsequent editions, following notification. The publishers are grateful to the following individuals and organizations for their permission to reproduce material on the following pages (t = top, b = bottom, l = left, r = right);

Cover Mary Evans Picture Library; **Endpapers, p1, 14-15, 16-17, 38-39, 48** © Historical picture archive/CORBIS; **p2-3, 6-7, 44-45, 46** © Historical picture archive/CORBIS; **p1** Mary Evans Picture Library; **p2** © Stapleton Collection/CORBIS; **p3** © Royalty-Free/CORBIS; **p4-5** © Royal Holloway and Bedford New College, Surrey, UK/Bridgeman Art Library; **p5 (t)** Mary Evans Picture Library; **p6 (l)** © Bettmann/CORBIS; **p6 (r)** Mary Evans Picture Library; **p7** Mary Evans Picture Library; **p8-9** © National Gallery Collection; By kind permission of the Trustees of the National Gallery, London/CORBIS; **p8 (t)** Mary Evans Picture Library; **p9 (t)** © Hulton-Deutsch Collection/CORBIS **p11** Mary Evans Picture Library; **p12** Mary Evans Picture Library; **p13 (t)** © Birmingham Museums and Art Gallery/Bridgeman Art Library; **p13 (b)** Mary Evans Picture Library; **p14-15** © The Art Archive/Tate Gallery London/Eileen Tweedy ; **p14 (t)** Mary Evans Picture Library; **p15 (t)** Mary Evans Picture Library; **p16** Mary Evans Picture Library; **p17 (t)** Mary Evans Picture Library; **p17 (b)** © FORBES Magazine Collection, New York, USA/Bridgeman Art Library; **p18-19** © John Ronayne/Geffrye Museum; **p19 (t)** Mary Evans Picture Library; **p20** Mary Evans Picture Library; **p21 (t)** Mary Evans Picture Librbary/The Women's Library; **p21 (b)** Getty Images; **p22-23** Heritage Images © Museum of London; **p22 (t)** Mary Evans Picture Library; **p23 (t)** Mary Evans Picture Library; **p24-25** © Paul Hardy/CORBIS; **p24 (b)** V&A Images/Victoria & Albert Museum; **p25 (b)** Heritage Images © The British Library ; **p26-27** © Historical Picture Archive/CORBIS; **p26 (t)** Mary Evans Picture Library; **p27 (t)** © Historical Picture Archive/CORBIS; **p28** Heritage Images © Science Museum, London; **p29 (t)** © Hulton-Deutsch Collection/CORBIS; **p29 (b)** © Archivo Iconografico, S.A./CORBIS; **p30-31** Getty Images; **p30 (t)** Heritage Images © National Railway Museum, York; **p31 (b)** Mary Evans Picture Library; **p32** Courtesy Woodfall Film Productions/RGA; **p33 (b)** Mary Evans Picture Library; **p34** ©Sean Sexton Collection/CORBIS; **p35 (t)** Mary Evans Picture Library; **p35 (b)** Mary Evans Picture Library; **p36-37** © Bettmann/CORBIS; **p36 (t)** © British Museum, London, UK/Bridgeman Art Library; **p37 (r)** © Bettmann/CORBIS; **p38-39** Mary Evans Picture Library; **p39 (t)** Mary Evans Picture Library; **p40-41** Mary Evans Picture Library; **p40 (t)** Heritage Images © Science Museum, London; **p41 (t)** Mary Evans Picture Library; **p42-43** © Stone; **p42 (t)** © Pawel Libera/CORBIS; **p43 (t)** © Hulton-Deutsch Collection/CORBIS; **p44-45** © The Art Archive/Tate Gallery London/Eileen Tweedy; **p45 (t)** Mary Evans Picture Library; **p46** © Keystone/Getty Images

Illustrations by Inklink Firenze and Ross Watton
Additional editorial material by Rachel Firth
Photoshop by Mike Olley and John Russell
Additional design by Lucy Owen

Index